Becoming a
Butterfly

FIRST EDITION

Editor Rachel Harrison; **Art Editor** Jane Horne; **Senior Editor** Linda Esposito;
Senior Art Editor Diane Thistlethwaite; **Pre-Production Producer** Nadine King;
Producer Sara Hu; **Picture Researcher** Frances Vargo; **Jacket Designer** Natalie Godwin;
Publishing Manager Bridget Giles; **Natural History Consultant** Theresa Greenaway;
Reading Consultant Linda Gambrell, PhD

THIS EDITION

Editorial Management by Oriel Square
Produced for DK by WonderLab Group LLC
Jennifer Emmett, Erica Green, Kate Hale, *Founders*

Editors Grace Hill Smith, Libby Romero, Maya Myers, Michaela Weglinski;
Photography Editors Kelley Miller, Annette Kiesow, Nicole DiMella;
Managing Editor Rachel Houghton; **Designers** Project Design Company;
Researcher Michelle Harris; **Copy Editor** Lori Merritt; **Indexer** Connie Binder;
Proofreader Larry Shea; **Reading Specialist** Dr. Jennifer Albro; **Curriculum Specialist** Elaine Larson

Published in the United States by DK Publishing
1745 Broadway, 20th Floor, New York, NY 10019
Copyright © 2023 Dorling Kindersley Limited
DK, a Division of Penguin Random House LLC
23 24 25 26 10 9 8 7 6 5 4 3 2 1
001-334105-July/2023

A catalog record for this book
is available from the Library of Congress.
HC ISBN: 978-0-7440-7489-5
PB ISBN: 978-0-7440-7491-8

DK books are available at special discounts when purchased in bulk for sales promotions, premiums,
fundraising, or educational use. For details, contact: DK Publishing Special Markets,
1745 Broadway, 20th Floor, New York, NY 10019
SpecialSales@dk.com

Printed and bound in China

The publisher would like to thank the following for their kind permission to reproduce their images:
a=above; c=center; b=below; l=left; r=right; t=top; b/g=background

Alamy Stock Photo: Nature Photographers Ltd / Robin Bush 16, Mervyn Rees 20, 21t, Malcolm Schuyl 19, Dave Watts 3cb;
Dreamstime.com: Adrian Eugen Ciobaniuc 24-25, Fotyma 22-23t, Anton Nikitinskiy 6b, Maciej Olszewski 24bl,
Sleepyhobbit 4-5; **Getty Images:** De Agostini / DEA / M. Giovanoli 10t; **Getty Images / iStock:** epantha 30cla, 30bl;
naturepl.com: Kim Taylor 22cla, 30tl; **Shutterstock.com:** Dan Bagur 14-15t, Bildagentur Zoonar GmbH 28-29,
jjvxphotography 26-27; **Warren Photographic Limited:** 12-13

Cover images: *Front:* **Dreamstime.com:** Sgoodwin4813 c/ (bc), Nina Sitkevich b, Sandra Standbridge ca;
Getty Images / iStock: epantha cb

All other images © Dorling Kindersley
For more information see: www.dkimages.com

For the curious
www.dk.com

Becoming a Butterfly

Karen Wallace

Contents

6   A Butterfly Mom

8   Caterpillar

14   Getting Bigger

18   Cozy Chrysalis

22   Happy Birthday, Butterfly!

28   A New Butterfly Mom

30   Glossary

31   Index

32   Quiz

A Butterfly Mom

A butterfly flits
from leaf to leaf.
Her red-striped wings
shine in the sun.
She touches the leaves
with her feet and
her feelers.

wings

feelers

egg

On each little leaf
she lays one or two eggs.
She squeezes the eggs
out of her body.
The outside
of each egg
is covered
with a shell.

shell

Caterpillar

A caterpillar grows inside each egg. Soon one is ready to hatch.

She hatches out
of her shell.
Then she munches the
leaves around her.

The caterpillar makes
a tent from a leaf.
She uses the tent to hide
from the birds, which are
sharp-eyed
and hungry.

Hundreds of caterpillars
hatch alongside her.
Some are unlucky.
Hungry birds peck them.
Furry bats snatch them.
Spiders catch them.

The caterpillar is hungry. She needs to eat so she crawls from her leaf tent. She climbs up strong stems and clings to young leaves.

The caterpillar munches and crunches all the leaves she can find.

Getting Bigger

The caterpillar gets bigger and bigger. Her black and yellow skin gets tighter and tighter.

Munch!
Crunch!

skin

Suddenly the skin starts to split open! The caterpillar wriggles out with a brand-new skin.

The caterpillar
grows quickly.
She sheds her skin
four times before
she is fully grown.

She looks for a
leaf that is sturdy
and strong.

She hangs upside down.

Cozy Chrysalis

The caterpillar is changing into a chrysalis (KRIS-uh-liss).

Outside, her skin turns hard to keep her safe.

Inside, something amazing is happening.

chrysalis

Then one day the
chrysalis splits open.

Something crawls out
into the sunshine.
It has a head and six legs.
It has wings and a body.
What can it be?

Happy Birthday, Butterfly!

A brand-new butterfly rests in the sunshine!

Her wings are soft.
They have been
squashed inside
the chrysalis.

The butterfly flits from flower to flower. She sucks up the sweet nectar with her long, hollow tongue. When she is not eating, her tongue is curled like a spring.

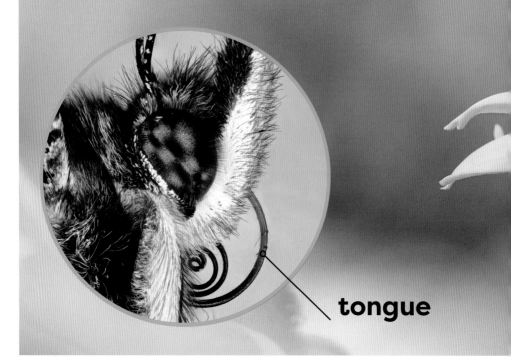

tongue

Now it is time
to look for a mate.
She finds him
sitting on a leaf.

They dance
in the sunshine
and fly
off together.

A New Butterfly Mom

The butterfly flits from flower to flower. Her red-striped wings shine in the sun.

She looks for a leaf
where she can lay
her eggs.

Glossary

chrysalis
the stage of growth
from caterpillar
to butterfly

feelers
what butterflies use to
touch their surroundings

shell
the hard outside
covering of an egg

skin
the outside layer
of a body

wings
what butterflies use
to fly

Index

bats   11

birds   10, 11

caterpillar   8, 10, 11, 12, 14, 15, 17, 18

chrysalis   18, 19, 21, 23

eggs   7, 8, 29

feelers   6

flower   24, 28

hatch   8, 9, 11

legs   21

mate   26

mom   6, 28

nectar   24

sheds   17

shell   7, 9

skin   14, 15, 17, 18

spiders   11

sun   6, 22, 27, 28

tent   10, 12

tongue   24

wings   6, 21, 23, 28

Quiz

Answer the questions to see what you have learned. Check your answers with an adult.

1. What covers the outside of each butterfly egg?

2. What does the caterpillar do after she hatches out of her shell?

3. What does a caterpillar make from a leaf?

4. How many times does a caterpillar shed its skin?

5. How many legs does a butterfly have?

1. A shell 2. She munches the leaves around her
3. A tent 4. Four 5. Six